It would be difficult to imagine a better moment in history for a book on the subject of discerning of spirits. With the current seemingly continual conflict between political ideologies, economic systems, gender identities and identity politics, sexual morays and the pervasive role of government in every area of life we must be able to see the world through God's eyes and act decisively and confidently by His grace.

Traditional mindsets will not show us how to live in these chaotic times. We must know God's will and to be able to articulate it against every vain philosophy and worldly orientation to be overcomers.

I heartily recommend April Stutzman's book, The Chronicles of a Discerner, as a helpful guide through the confusing maze of modern demonic agendas that besiege today's professing Christians at every turn.

Joan Hunter Author/Healing Evangelist

host Miracles Happen TV show

Wow...this book is a great simple read!! April's experiences were the Holy Spirits soil for His seeds to grow and mature her in this gift. She is precise and teaches along the way, as she navigates through her journey. This is an anointed and very necessary book in the hour we are living in. I highly recommend it!!

Constance J. Bounds

Gods Eagles Ministry

What others are saying about April Stutzman and The Chronicles of a Discerner

If you are one seeking to be mentored in the things of the Spirit the good news is you hold in your hand the priceless personal insights of one who has gone before you. In this book April Stutzman reveals her very personal journey of discovery into the Discerning of Spirits. Not many people are prepared to share what you will read here for fear of being ridiculed, thought strange or a misfit. However, if you have ever picked up thoughts that were not your own, received unexplainable feelings on certain part of your body or sensed or seen angels then its likely you were operating in the discerning of spirits. April provides wisdom in how she learned to navigate these experiences. The sad truth is many misunderstand these glimpses into the world of spirits around them and consequently fail to reach the fullness of their spiritual potential. Discerning of spirits is a complementary gift and for that reason it is often overlooked. However, this gift of the Holy Spirit enhances and fine tunes all the other gifts including: deliverance, counsel, dream interpretation and the delivery of prophecy. This is a timely and an easy-to-read journey of discovery that will add years of experience and broaden your personal understanding into the multi-faceted voice of God's Spirit.

Adrian Beale and Adam F Thompson
Authors of The Divinity Code to Understanding your
Dreams and Visions
thedivinitycode.org

As the need for discernment increases in this hour, many are becoming aware they carry this gifting of discerning of spirits. The Chronicles of A Discerner is a great book that introduces, breaks down, and gives articulation to this gift. This a great tool for any level, but especially those stepping into the gifting of discerning of spirits. Those growing in this gift will gain a greater confidence and gain a greater assurance they're not alone in this gifting. It's normal!

Madeline James, founder of Madeline James Ministries, and author of Unlocking Your Prophetic Voice

Chronicles of a Discerner is a practical yet powerful guide that will help you gain an understanding of the gift of discernment in greater depths. April walks you through her own personal journey of this unique gift and shares how she grew "spiritual muscles" to carry the weight of what the Lord has shown her over the years of cultivating a beautiful and personal relationship with the Holy Spirit. April also helps you to navigate what you may already be experiencing or will experience in your own life and calling. Not only will this book give you language, but it will also stir up a hunger to go after an intimate relationship with the Spirit of the Living God and to partner with Him in everything that you discern. Get ready to learn how to walk out this gift in the love of the Father!

Teryn Yancey, Co-Founder of Glory Culture International

April Stutzman has written a book about discernment that is not a theological dissertation but birthed from the fires of trial. God has raised up his daughter as a prophetic voice to impart to the nations of the world. This teaching comes from many personal battles that she has fought and won. I heard a minister say that the Word of God is not on trial; because the Word of the Lord will try us like the Word tried Joseph before he became prime minister of the entire world. This is the work that you hold in your hand.a life that is being tried through the gift of discernment. This gift will deliver us from death as we yield to the Holy Ghost. April Stutzman has this assignment as a prophetic deliverer to help free the people of God from demonic bondages. This book will help you understand pitfalls and principles as the gift of discernment is developed through usage. This book will enlighten and validate your walk in the Spirit as the gift of discernment increases in the glory.

Apostle Clinton C. Baker Co-Founder of Valiant

Ministries International, Inc.

I highly recommend April's new book, The Chronicles of a Discerner. April is a extraordinary discerner and uses extravagant wisdom in discerning. The tips April shares in this book are a blessing to all who read it. Teaching any level discerner to stretch and grow. Pulling you to a higher level of discerning of spirits in the days we are living in.

Joanna Beck Ministries

THE CHRONICLES

OF A

DISCERNER

THE CHRONICLES OF A DISCERNER

How to grow spiritual muscle in discerning

April Stutzman

ISBN: 13-978-1-7351751-0-2

Library of Congress Control Number: 2020915940

Audible: Audible, Amazon, and Itunes, other platforms

Dedication

I dedicate this book to the **Holy Spirit**. He is a person and I honor Him. I would not be where I am today if He had not cooperated with what the Father wanted for me, and supernaturally healed the wounds of my soul. I owe You my life, Holy Spirit, and I say thank you! You're the lover of my soul.

To my **husband, Richard,** who is the love of my life and has believed and supported me since day one. I am so thankful for your support daily, and to be able to move with the Holy Spirit as you cheer me on! You're my best friend. Thank you, Jesus, for bringing us together. One of the best days of my life was when I married you.

To my **kids,** whom I love with all my heart. As I stand back and watch the Lord restore the years that the enemy has stolen from us, may my ceiling be your floor!

Contents

Foreword

April Stutzman is a powerful and solid voice with a timely teaching for the Body of Christ.

It is the charge of the five-fold minister to equip the body of Christ – for ministry, edification, and the unity of the faith. (Ephesians 4) Chronicles of a Discerner was written by an anointed equipper and discerner for such a time as this! Discernment is a pivotal gift that the Church cannot afford to overlook. Do not discount the importance of the book you hold in your hands, or the gift that it imparts.

In the book of Malachi we read, "Then you shall again discern between the righteous and the wicked, between one who serves God, and one who does not serve Him." (Malachi 3:18 NKJV)

If you cannot discern, how will you know? And if you do not know, how will you keep from being deceived? The gift of Discerning of Spirits is of utmost importance.

Matthew 24 says, "For false christs and false prophets will rise and show great signs and wonders to deceive, if possible, even the elect. See, I have told you beforehand." (Matthew 24:24-25 NKJV)

April is a next generation leader whose teaching has a tail – like a powerful horse running swiftly by, tail elegantly swishing back and forth, while you hardly notice that it strikes each target with precision as it swings to the left and the right. April's ministry focuses on training up the body of Christ to run the last-days race with perseverance, well equipped and advancing in unity as the army of Jesus Christ. Breeding well-fed warriors who have eaten the meat of the Word and memorized the battle strategies.

As you read Chronicles of a Discerner, or study under April Stutzman in any of her classes, you will have your senses trained in discernment as the Word of God encourages every believer to do. She does not mince words or hold back – she lays it out straight and encourages every believer to come up higher!

April writes, "I hope to help you recognize your gift and how to partner with God in it. I want you to know you are not crazy when you see or sense what others do not!" It is refreshing to read a book that is not only instructional and empowering, but also transparent and easy to read. Chronicles of a Discerner is filled with prayers and impartation, as well as clear steps to navigate this powerful gift.

It is my great pleasure to recommend Chronicles of a Discerner by April Stutzman.

."...He gives someone else the ability to discern whether a message is from the Spirit of God or from another spirit." (1 *Cor. 12:10 NLT)*

Pastor Jodi Ahrens-Ferguson

Co-Founder of Warriors Heart Ministry

YouTube: Signs Following with JC

Introduction

So I am a discerner, now what? Maybe that was your question as you picked up this book. Perhaps you are more mature in discernment and surprised that someone has written about it, but you are reading it out of curiosity. Either way, the Holy Spirit is going to meet you where you are! Holy Spirit has something amazing in store for you, to help you navigate this gift. I feel His heart on it. Many discerners have had the gift since birth but have been unsure of what they carry. They have been misunderstood, isolated, and rejected. So, before we unwrap what the Holy Spirit desires to say to you about this gift, set aside your questions and speak aloud this prayer:

"Holy Spirit give me fresh revelation on discernment, and the grace and love to walk it out. Help me to partner with you in love and humility. When I discern something and do not know what to do, help me to receive your wise counsel, and lean into your understanding. I also ask, Holy Spirit, that you

would bring into my life other discerners who have your heart."

Now, get ready to watch as Holy Spirit journeys with you and teaches you to navigate this gift in a whole new way. We will begin to unravel what discernment is; its pitfalls, and how to handle it with purity and strength.

I don't mean to dishonor this amazing gift from God, but I have to say it has taken me through the school of hard knocks. I believe that everyone who carries this gift wants to give up at some point. At different stages they have wanted to lay it down and walk away. Even now, there are days when I think those thoughts. It's the very reason I wrote this book. I want to share some of the process it takes to walk in this gifting and I hope to encourage you and come alongside you as you grow. I love you for being brave enough to pick up this book. It shows your desire to grow your gift. That desire is the stepping stone to your higher level because Holy Spirit will impart to you as you read.

I must emphasize that discernment is a gift from the Holy Spirit. It is *not* an occultic gift, where people follow their carnal agendas to bring harm, or to accomplish selfish, witchcraft desires. The occult can only counterfeit God's original design to use our senses in understanding the spirit world. And God's design is always through the lens of Jesus Christ and the Holy Spirit, who are not only supernatural but also have the heart of the Father. If you have previously dabbled in the occult because you were so hungry for the supernatural, just repent now. Say aloud, *Jesus I repent for dabbling in or being involved with* _____. *Please forgive me. Set me free, Holy Spirit, and show me what you have for my life.* If you prayed that prayer, expect to be delivered by the Lord, for He is much more powerful and creative than any counterfeit.

God intended the supernatural to operate from His glory realm and to be walked out in love. Anything that is walked out apart from God, Jesus, and the Holy Spirit, is a counterfeit.

If this is new to you and you have never asked Jesus Christ into your heart, you can pray the following prayer aloud: *Jesus, I believe you died on the cross for my sins (missing the mark of Your high calling on my life). Please come into my heart. I repent for all the things I have done and invite you in my heart to make me a new man/woman. Holy Spirit reveal yourself to me and fill me with your presence. Your word says that if I Seek first the kingdom of God everything, I need shall be given to me (*Matthew 6:33) NKJV.

This is the true freedom of new life in Him. Now that we have established the foundation of who this gift comes from, let's dive into walking it out.

What Is Discerning of Spirits?

What is discerning of spirits and where is it in the Bible? Discernment is mentioned numerous times, but let's focus on where it is spoken of as a gift given by the Holy Spirit. Underline it in your Bible. 1 Corinthians 12:1-10 lists a number of spiritual gifts, including 'discerning of spirits'. Perhaps you have read that verse many times but overlooked that particular line? Perhaps you skipped over the whole verse because you had no idea what it meant? Be honest, there's no judgment here! There was a time when I had no understanding of its meaning, let alone that I would walk in it in my own life. There are more scriptures on this subject throughout the book but, for those who are new to it, let's dive into the very basics of this gift.

The Wikipedia dictionary describes discernment as: 'The ability to obtain sharp perceptions or to judge well.[1] A discerning individual is considered to possess wisdom, and to be of good judgment, especially so with regard to a subject matter often overlooked by others.' If even a secular dictionary defines discernment this way, don't you think it's something to be desired? I love how Jennifer Eivaz describes this gift because it is so true: 'This gift is a sensory process before an intellectual one. In a Greek-thinking culture that elevates logic and reason above emotions and the spiritual, we have inadvertently shut down the internal mechanism by which this gift flows.[2] This shows why many in the body of Christ have not understood or valued this gift.

Why is this gift neglected and less supported than other gifts? I believe it is because the doctrine of cessation has created a fear of the supernatural. Central to cessationism is the belief that spiritual gifts, such as speaking in tongues, prophecy and healing, all stopped at the end of the apostolic age. Cessationism is the opposite of continuationism, which teaches that the Holy Spirit continues to give spiritual gifts to people in every era.

The senses that God himself gave you are not just for relating to human beings, but also for communicating with *Him*! I love for Papa to talk to me whatever way He chooses, whether from the Bible, an inner sense of His voice, a dream, trance, vision, or by discerning. All of those ways of communication are found in the Bible. God is not limited in the ways that He speaks to us.

Let His glory flood you right now as you read this. Just say, *'Lord I repent for all the times I have only used my senses to be earthly minded. Right now, I dedicate all my senses to you, Holy Spirit. I surrender my natural sight, hearing, smelling, touch, and taste to you. Please activate my spiritual senses in each of them. Thank you, Jesus!'*

I encourage you to watch what happens this week as you open your senses to allow God to communicate to you through them. Do all those things that build your relationship with the Lord - fast, soak, pray, worship - but allow Him to expand and activate your senses while you are doing that. Allow Holy Spirit to impart to you the gift of discerning of spirits and teach you to co-labor with him. As with any gift, you will need to steward it well. In the beginning, you may try to figure out in your mind what is going on without leaning into the Holy Spirit. You will find this to be frustrating. Let me make it plain; nothing is to replace the Holy Spirit in the use of this gift. As you lean into Holy Spirit, you will become more and more sensitive to what He is showing you.

Another thing to be aware of is that - just as with any other gift - there are different measures. In the same way that a healing minister may carry a particular grace for a specific condition, a discerner may have more grace and discernment in specific areas than others. The important thing is that you do not compare yourself to others. God made you unique for a reason. Rejoice in that. This is your journey, not anyone else's, and you answer to God alone.

Journey with joy in God and trust His ability more than fearing the devil's ability to deceive you. Some of you will be surprised to realize how often you have been hearing from God. You may have been operating in this gift all your life and worried that you were losing your mind! Some people have been misjudged and labeled as unstable or "strange" because no one came alongside them to encourage and teach them how to steward this gift. I am so excited to see more books on this subject being written for the body of Christ. They have never been more needed than in this present time. I do not claim to know everything there is to know about this subject, because God is always unfolding revelation, but I do hope to encourage you by sharing my journey. I hope to help you recognize your gift and how to partner with God in it. I want you to know you are not crazy when you see or sense what others do not!

I want you to know, too, that you are not alone. Without mature support in place, it can be a heavyweight to carry what you see. I believe discerners benefit from being in community with other discerners, either online, or as part of a small group, locally. Do whatever it takes to connect with other discerners. I see a breed of people coming out of the woodwork, as it were, who will walk high in the gift of discerning of spirits because God is raising up an army of deliverers.

Everyone has a natural intuition - that hidden gut-feeling - but discerning of spirits is on a different level. Everyone has a distinct discerning gift. We develop our own individual patterns of its 'language' so that we receive meanings through our various senses. Each person is uniquely designed in the way their spirit communicates to their body. I call it a signal, or a discerning-of-spirits language. There are certain signals that my body gives me, depending on what I am discerning. Let me encourage you; you will learn to read your own signals.

You may be asking how this works. Let's take your natural senses and apply them to the spirit world. You might *see* angels, **hear** demons, **smell** principalities, **hug** a person to discern their heart, and **taste** the honey of the revelation of God. As James Goll says, we just know things in our knower; you know something to be true, and your stomach bears witness to the truth. You could say that this gift causes you to live in Hebrews 5:14, *"But solid food is for the mature, who because of **practice** have their senses trained to discern good and evil."* Discerning is solid food. It is not for the babe and the weak at heart. God trusts you to take time to train your senses and to come into maturity in this gift.

"I declare over you, right now, a fresh oil to wash over you, releasing discernment. Lord, for those who already walk

in this gift, I declare increase and a fresh grace over them, in Jesus name."

The world doesn't value spiritual things, only carnal ones, therefore they do not see past the natural cares of this world. It should be our priority to see what heaven is doing and intentionally partner with the Holy Spirit so that we can walk into a room and distinguish what spirits are there. How can we be about our Father's business if we have not trained our spiritual senses to know what He is doing?

At this point, you may be saying, 'I am at the beginning of this learning process, and I am feeling overwhelmed!' That is precisely why I am sharing some of my experiences in the growth process. Remember, I am still growing, too. This gift increases in me daily and goes to new levels so that I am continually having to rely on my trusty friend, the Holy Spirit. The Bible says, *"But the Helper, the Holy Spirit, whom the Father will send in My name, He will teach you all things, and bring to remembrance all that I said to you."* (John 14:26 NASB). He *teaches* you all things. This includes how to walk out your gift of distinguishing, or discerning, of spirits (abbreviated from here on, to DOS, for convenience sake). The Holy Spirit wants you to understand how this gift flows so He can help you accomplish the Father's will on the earth.

The Holy Spirit wants me to declare such precision to your DOS right now. *"Papa, in this season, I decree and declare to those reading this, that precision is happening in their gift. Their discernment will be razor-sharp! We cut off, right now, every assignment of error or mixture to contaminate the gift in Jesus name. The wind of the Holy Spirit is present with you to move you into the new and help you let go of any staleness of the last season. I sense for some people that the disappointment that they have felt in the past has hindered their gift. I command all disappointment to go, all heaviness be gone now, in Jesus name. All sorrow and grief go! I release the joy of the Lord and ask you, Papa God, to send the ministering angels to them."*

Maybe you are one of those who has experienced the enemy using your gift against you. You have been falsely labeled as bipolar, or something similar, because you have seen and heard things that most people do not. I am not saying there is never a bipolar chemical imbalance that is needing to be healed, but I do say some highly gifted people have been labeled instead of supported. They have not received help to navigate the spiritual world in a healthy way. The Holy Spirit showed me that many people needing labels cut off would pick up this book. I cut false labels off you! Right now, do something physical to demonstrate removing that label off your mind. Do that as a prophetic act. Say, "I am set free from any false labels. I am a child of the Most High God, and God loves and values me." In Jesus name, I agree with you, and break off every assignment of misunderstanding, and declare healing over your heart, right now. Hallelujah, God is a God of restoration!

In the next chapter, we will get into some things you may go through as you walk out this gift.

Help, What Do I Feel?

How often have you asked that question, 'What do I feel'? Well, welcome to DOS! I believe all beginners ask this question many times in the process of learning to train their senses. I know I did! Do not feel alone in this. You're not crazy; you're just carrying a gift.

I see the Holy Spirit right now is awakening memories in someone who was conscious of this gift as a child. The enemy tried to shut it down. He tried to make you think you were crazy. I break that fear off you, right now, in the name of Jesus. As you are reading this, memories are coming back of times you discerned correctly. Holy Spirit is encouraging you and validating you. Do not shut down the gift; just learn to harness it.

Let me give you a few examples of how this works as you start out. Firstly, there are different categories of DOS. You may distinguish human spirits, angelic spirits, demons, and the Holy Spirit. This is where you need to navigate closely with Holy Spirit, because there is a learning curve just as there is a learning curve in riding a bike. You want to become balanced so that you have a healthy perspective in every situation.

I decree and declare over you that you will navigate with Holy Spirit to distinguishing healthily in each category. You will not distinguish just one or the other but will distinguish all. It's like a healthy diet. It takes a little bit of meat, a little bit of potatoes, vegetables, fats, and so forth. Unfortunately, in my case, in the beginning of this gifting, I distinguished more human spirits and the demonic because of all the trauma I had been through. You can read about that in my first book, *Gateway to my Miracle*.[1]

Let me describe a situation you may have experienced:

You are sitting in a cinema, for example, with your family, and watching a movie. Suddenly, you keep hearing thoughts out of nowhere in your head, "*Man, why doesn't this guy love me? Well, no one has ever loved me. Why do I even try, why am I even on this date?*" These thoughts are speaking loudly in your head, and you can't understand why you are thinking them. You shake it off and hope that no one has seen you freaking out about it. You regain your composure, glance at your family, hoping they haven't notice anything odd, and refocus on the movie and the story line. Then suddenly, you start hearing these thoughts again. *"I just wish someone would love me and treat me right. Why am I always going out with no-hopers? Why can't I find a decent man."* Once again, you are freaking out, confused. You know you are happily married, watching a movie with your husband and kids; these thoughts shouldn't be happening! The enemy of your soul is telling you you're crazy, and you're thinking, "I am not telling anyone about this because they *will* think I am nuts. My husband would tell me I haven't had enough sleep or something. I have no language to *explain* what just happened, much less understand it." So you try to shut it down and ignore it and convince yourself that you are okay. Eventually, the movie ends, and you leave the cinema, relieved that the thoughts have gone away.

Welcome to the gift of distinguishing of spirits! In that movie theatre, you were picking up on another person's thoughts. You were distinguishing a human spirit. Let me give you an example from scripture. In Luke 5:22 NKJV, we read, *"But when Jesus perceived their thoughts, he answering them said unto them, Why are you reasoning in your hearts?"*

Distinguishing the thoughts of a human spirit is part of the gifting. You were picking up another person's thought at the movie theatre, but you were unable to distinguish between those thoughts and your own. The other person's thoughts were so loud to you that they overwhelmed you. The key to this part of the gift is to know yourself. If the thoughts you are hearing are not things you would say to yourself, then they probably belong to someone else in the room. This is where you start navigating this gift, and you ask, "Holy Spirit, why am I hearing the thoughts of that person?" He showed you for a reason, and if He took the time to show you this, it is important to Him. He may instruct you to pray for that person to be freed from thoughts of rejection, and that they find the right marriage partner. Or, He may tell you to pray they come to faith in Jesus so they find the true love they are searching for and which can only be found in Him.

This is the key to navigating this part of the gift - rely on God, not your human reasoning. Sometimes thoughts are so loud you may feel like they are invading your space. As you grow in this, I promise it will get easier. As Jennifer Eivaz says, "You gain muscles over time."[2] I do not say any of these things lightly. I am convinced this gift takes true grit and stamina, and the maturity to rely on the Holy Spirit for help.

My experience of maturing in this gift has been a true roller coaster ride. I would love to say it was all peachy and roses, but I'd be lying. The truth is, it has been a process. I have grown in this gift only by the grace of the Holy Spirit, good mentors, impartations, and the times when my more structured husband has kept me balanced. He kept me grounded at those time when my emotions became intense, and I felt things so deeply. As soon as we married there was a huge increase in this gift, and I am not sure he was quite ready for that! God was faithful, though, and from the beginning, my husband has always relied on Christ to support me.

Wild, crazy stuff would happen over and over again. It comes with the gift, it's part of the mantle of it. You are a great threat to the enemy, so He hates this gift. He is afraid of what you carry, so he will throw all kinds of stupid stuff at you. I have had clairvoyants just appear in my bedroom. A witch would manifest and try to give me a potion. I had to learn to discern who and what these manifestations were, and shut them down. This is why it is so important you keep your eyes on Jesus, so you are not worn out from battling these attacks.

Psalm 91 says we hide in the shadow of His wings. Sometimes after overcoming a great battle with this gift, it is time to go hide in God's presence and soak - which means, you worship Him until you find yourself in the shelter of His glory. Remember Isaiah 54:17: "No weapon formed against you will prosper...." (NASB) No weapon *means* no weapon. Trust me, with this gift, there will be many weapons formed but none will prosper. You will expose the enemy and become a strategist with this gift. You can see what is hidden, and that makes you an uncommon opponent. Where we can see and overturn, is where we want to be. May the Lord Jesus Christ train us to take the offensive, and not respond to the low blows the enemy tries to throw. I sometimes had times of great battles until the discerning radar hit the mark. The Holy Spirit would highlight the true issue, and I would pray the Word and stand. As soon as Holy Spirit revealed the source of the attack, victory would come. I love that about the Holy Spirit. He makes you an overcomer in all things because of Jesus Christ.

The roller-coaster of learning takes you on many ups and downs. On a particular day, you may be practicing discerning good and evil - as the word says in Hebrews 5:14 – and you realize you can't decide *what* you're feeling. That's okay, just take a deep breath and trust God to walk you through it. Sometimes it can be overwhelming just to walk down a crowded street, because you see and feel so much emotion from the people around you.

Here is a typical scenario: you accept an invitation to attend a party, and you expect to have a happy time relaxing with friends. You're fine for the first 15 minutes. You get a plate of food and sit down to eat, and suddenly you have a feeling of dread. You start hearing in your head, *'Man, that woman is beautiful, I wish I could undress her.'* You freak out; oh my gosh, what was I thinking? You calm yourself down and remind yourself you're not crazy, but then you hear, *'I wonder what color panties she has on.'* Suddenly, you realize: I'm a woman. I don't think like that or act like that. Where is this coming from? Holy Spirit then draws your attention to the man across the room who has a demon of perversion. Two spirits that DOS people are really sensitive to are perversion and witchcraft. They really try to wear you out.

Now it all makes sense. You were discerning how that demon was using him. What if this happened, but Holy Spirit said nothing about it to you? You would have to put it on a shelf. At that point, it's important just to remind yourself it's par for the course with the gift of discernment. Know your own norm or baseline. Things you would not say or do. As the gift grew in me, I could pick out anyone in the room who had perversion because I felt it so strongly. But even though Holy Spirit had shown me, I had to walk it out in love. I had to listen to Holy Spirit to know whether I was required to pray for the person and declare their freedom or just take it as a warning to be aware. Either way, I had to love and use wisdom. All the gifts of God are for redemption. They do not give you the right to judge anything about that person. You have to keep a pure heart with this gift. You can very quickly become cynical and hard unless you daily ask the Father to help you know what to do with what you discern.

What if that same man was perverted because he had been raped as a kid? Would you still judge him? We are called to love regardless of what we are discerning. Even if the man had a spirit of perversion because he was sleeping around, it is not our place to judge. Maybe you were shown that perverted spirit so you could repent for the man so Holy Spirit could deal with his heart. Regardless, get your heart right before the Lord, because your sensitivity to this spirit will have you encountering it often.

Let's talk about another spirit you may have trouble

figuring out at first. I am making up some of the scenarios to protect people, but this stuff does happen. For example, you're sitting in church, and someone takes the seat immediately in front of you. Suddenly, your nervous system explodes to a level ten. You are really irritated, angry, or frustrated. You pray the person moves somewhere else. You try to get a handle on it, but it's overwhelming. Now you start to cough (remember everyone's body signals are different?). Welcome to discerning witchcraft. People with the gift of DOS can usually smell that thing miles away! You will be sensitive to anyone who needs deliverance from a controlling spirit, jezebel spirit, or occultism. This gift is given particularly for the purpose of getting people delivered, but you have to ask Holy Spirit why He allowed *you* to perceive that thing and what is *your* assignment in it.

Some days it will be easy to discern correctly and some days your senses may be overloaded. Stay humble and ask your support community or mentor to help you, or call a trusted friend who can pray for you until you figure out why your discerning radar went wild. As you mature, the days you feel overloaded will lessen. In the process, get equipped and use wisdom strategies like the ones I have described. Study the subject, grow, and watch how the Holy Spirit gives you your own signals.

What do you I mean by 'signals'? I will give you an example; when my neck hurts in a certain spot I know it indicates something in particular to me. If my ear rings I know it means something else. When I feel a certain sensation on my right arm I know the Holy Spirit is highlighting a specific matter to me. When I begin to cough a lot the Holy Spirit is showing me another issue. There is a comprehensive list of how the Holy Spirit gave me different discerning signals and it took time to develop my understanding of what each of them meant. Don't get discouraged if your left foot goes numb around certain people! Ask the Holy Spirit what he wants to communicate through your senses (Hebrews 5:14). I suggest you keep a journal to record the different things that happen to you, so you can pick up on any patterns. It's like decoding a secret, intimate and unique language between you and the Holy Spirit. He teaches you every time you are brave enough to take this journey with him and discern that new spirit. He is training you for kingdom purposes. Be excited, He is trusting you with an amazing gift.

Remember every gift of the Holy Spirit is used for love and redemption. Love should flow out of this gift so the kingdom can be advanced. People can be set free; lives can be touched, and you can work with the Holy Spirit with heaven's agenda in mind. Many times, you may see something you don't want to see, and that is hard to bear. For example, you are so excited to re-connect with a friend you haven't seen in years. She suggested your favorite restaurant, so you meet her there. You feel so blessed to be able to fellowship together after so much time has passed. You start sharing with each other how much the Lord has done and you celebrate His goodness. Suddenly, you see the motives of her heart and know that she is regularly cheating on her husband and is even thinking about the guy right now. Ouch. Not what you wanted to see. Now you have to ask Holy Spirit whether to pray for her or confront her about it? Those are the situations no one prepares you for. You have to learn to navigate with the Holy Spirit. Even everyday situations take on a different appearance because you are discerning the hidden things of the spirit world. You begin to realize that your sensitivity to certain sights, sounds, smells, or environments, is your way of discerning issues in the spirit world. It is important not to mistake mere suspicion for discernment.

I find personal experience is often the best way to teach on this gift, so here is another example that I hope is helpful. You have been invited to a married couple's house for dinner. As you sit at the table you sense in your body a lot of tension and you feel strife running through your veins. You are conscious it is a tense environment. You begin to pray in your heart, asking the Lord to release His presence into that home. Within a few minutes you do not feel that tension anymore and you relax. Later, in the course of conversation, you discover that a neighbor visited that home two days before and brought with her a spirit of strife that stayed. They had been under attack by this spirit ever since. Yes, that can happen, but you can only shift things if you discern the spirit of the matter.

You will see what others do not see even when it's right under their noses, but it is so important you do not get into pride with this gift. People with the gift of DOS would be wise to have around them other people with this gift. Only God sees and hears all. There could be something right under our nose that we miss, because it was not our assignment and therefore Holy Spirit did not give us the signals. Sometimes our flesh really doesn't *want* to see it, and we ignore the signals in our mind because we really *like* the person standing in front of us and we don't want to know anything negative about them. It happens to the best of Discerners. Also, be prepared to thank the person who reveals something for your own, or your ministry's, protection, that you might have missed.

You may be asking, "How will I ever learn to manage this gift?" Settle it in your heart once and for all that you will only ever manage this gift in the power of the Holy Spirit. The word says, "I can do all things through Him who strengthens me." (Phil. 4:13 NKJV) Learn to manage the gift not by turning it off or shutting it down, but by navigating all things with Him. Some of the most frustrating times for me and other DOS people I know, is when we have discerned something really heavy but we cannot figure out the source. Be patient with yourself. Stay at peace. Be reassured, peace like a river will help you flow no matter what you discern or what's going on around you. Christ speaks to your heart to say, "No evil will befall you; my angels have charge concerning you" (Psalms 91: 10,11) NKJV. His promises are true, and we can take them to the bank, as the saying has it.

No matter which stage you are in with your DOS gift -

beginner, intermediate, or walking very highly in it - trust the Holy Spirit for more. Remember there is no formula with this gift; you really must stay intimate with the Holy Spirit, cultivating a healthy relationship with Him. I believe, at this point, that it is so important to repeat that each person with DOS is unique in their gifting. You may have a unique grace for bloodline deliverance, or a unique grace for land deliverance, the list is endless.

Freely I have received, freely I give. In the name of Jesus Christ I impart to you more of the gift of discerning of spirits, and declare the grace over you to carry it well. Thank you, Holy Spirit for imparting to each person who is reading this book, so that an army of your people will be raised to walk with integrity in DOS.

I am excited for you. I can feel the Holy Spirit's heart for you right now. He loves to give good gifts. Get ready to see and sense things that you have never sensed before, and to have joy in the process, no matter how long the learning curve is. Choose Joy. You will mature as you practice.

Practice means *repeated exercise in or performance of an activity or skill so as to maintain proficiency in it.* The Lord showed me it is just like riding a bike. It takes time to develop the skill and the balance, but once you develop it, it becomes easier, and - like riding a bike - it gets smoother over time. You are blessed if you have a mentor in this gift or a friend who walks high in it. They will advise you in love. It helps to bounce things off them as you grow. You could call them and say, "I was at such and such place today and I saw such and such"- whether it be angel or a human spirit you discerned. Bounce it off your mentor. They will either say, "yes that's it" or put you on the right track and encourage you to keep practicing.

Lord I pray for the people reading this that you will give them strategic friendships that will help them grow in this gift and calling, and that their maturing may be accelerated for such a time as this in the kingdom. I decree and declare acceleration with precision, in Jesus name.

Discerning the Angels

I believe angels show up in many ways. Sometimes they are discernible by our natural senses, but sometimes we are not aware of who and what they are. The Bible tells us, *"We should not neglect hospitality to strangers, for by this some have entertained angels without knowing it"* (Hebrews 13:2, NASB). I have started with this part of DOS because, it was so much fun for me! I loved it because it allowed me to cooperate with heaven very effectively. I am often asked where it's mentioned in the Bible that people discern angels. The Bible texts quoted in the next paragraph make it plain that discerning of angels was a normal part of the Christian walk. The Bible also makes it plain, in 1 Corinthians 12:1-10, that discerning those angelic visitations is a gift from God.

Are angels discerned through DOS or the natural eye? Remembering that we see with the eyes of our heart, according to Ephesians 1:18, let's look at some places in scripture where the gift of discerning may be operating. In Luke 22: 41-43, an angel of the Lord appeared to Jesus and strengthened him. Jesus discerned the angel was there and it was a great benefit to Him. In Luke 1: 26 -38, Gabriel appeared to Mary and spoke to her about conceiving and giving birth to the one who was sent to be Messiah. In John 20: 11-13 Mary Magdalene saw two angels (perhaps with her spiritual eyes) sitting where the body of Jesus had been laid. In Luke 1: 11 an angel of the Lord appeared to Zechariah in the temple, standing on the right side of the altar of incense. When Zechariah saw him, fear fell upon him. By *seeing* the angel and *hearing* that he was to have a son who would herald the Messiah, Zechariah might be said to have both discerned and perceived. Did Zachariah see in the spirit or with the natural eye? In this case, the Bible does not say.

I repeat, if we did not need the gift of DOS why would Holy Spirit give it? If angels are seen in the spirit realm, wouldn't we need a spiritual gift to see them? Another example of this is in Acts when an angel appeared to Philip the evangelist and commanded him to travel to Gaza. *"Now an angel of the Lord spoke to Phillip, saying, 'Arise and go toward the south along the road which goes down from Jerusalem to Gaza."'* (Acts 8:26 NKJV) In Acts 10:3 NKJV we read, *"About the ninth hour of the day he [Cornelius] saw clearly in a vision (*does not say naked eye, so was it DOS?) *an angel of God coming and saying, Cornelius!"* meaning that an angelic being appeared to a Roman centurion, telling him to seek out the apostle Peter. In Acts 27:22-24, the angel of the Lord appeared to Paul to give him a message that no one would die on the ship he was sailing in. There are several other accounts of angels in the New Testament, and many in the Old Testament. You can study them yourself. You can consult with the Holy spirit as to which ones were seen with natural eyes and which were seen by DOS!

The discerning of angels was not the first part of DOS that was opened to me, although I wish it had been. Typically, but not always, people with this gift start with discerning the demonic. This happens because they tend to have suffered many unnecessary attacks on their life due to the very call and nature of this gift. I just want to make you aware. If you are operating in this gift and want to be more discerning of angels, ask the Holy Spirit for help so that He can transition you to seeing more of angels than demons. With most people it begins with a balance between the two, but then, as you mature, you will discern angels more readily than demons. However, it is true that some with this gift are graced from day one to discern the angelic. That's why this book is called A Chronicle because I use my own history to describe the diverse ways DOS may begin and then flow in our lives. As I have said regarding the healing gift, or miracles, or deliverance, everyone will have their own unique story of how the gift grew and matured.

I feel the heart of Holy Spirit right now. Some of you need to hear this, so just take a few minutes to receive this from Holy Spirit. I honor *your* story - and so does the Holy Spirit - of your journey in discerning of spirits. If your transition into this gift was tough and hard to handle, know that I celebrate with you for how far you have come in it with Holy Spirit. Today is a new day, and in Jesus name I declare a new grace over you to carry this gift.

I was probably discerning angels even as a small child, but my first clear adult memory of this was in a church service when I was in my thirties. I was standing and worshipping the Lord, lost in Him, when I suddenly saw angels flying over our heads. I saw them not with my natural eyes, but through the gift of discerning of spirits. I was shocked. I saw about five of them flying back and forth, with purpose, from the front of the church to the back of the congregation. I looked around to see if anyone else was staring up at them, seeing what I was seeing. I expected people to be pointing at what I was seeing. But when I realized no one was noticing anything, I thought I was losing my mind. I rubbed my eyes and still they were flying around. I was conscious of the presence of Holy Spirit so I was not afraid or concerned that what I was seeing was in any way bad, but it was new to me, and I didn't know what it meant or what I was to do with it.

I fell back on my friend, Holy Spirit, the counselor and teacher of all things. How I honor Him. My logical mind knew those angels were there, and I wanted to know why. At this time, I did not have much revelation in DOS. I was at a church where only a few of the gifts of the Holy Spirit manifested. The gift of discerning of spirits and deliverance was neither mentioned or taught in this church. I had no grid for what I was seeing. Even as I write this I am laughing with joy at the goodness of the Lord. He gives good gifts even when we have never heard of them and don't know what to do with them.

As I continued to watch those angels flying back and forth, the Holy Spirit spoke to my heart to say that the heavens were open and the angels were there to do whatever the people needed. At that moment I understood that whatever we would ask for under this open heaven we could receive. Healing, a miracle, or breakthrough, we would receive it. Amazed at what the Holy Spirit had told me, I ran to the pastor during the meet-and- greet break. I excitedly shared with him that the angels were here and that Holy Spirit told me they would do anything the congregation needed. I knew the pastor believed in angels because he had referred to them occasionally, although he never said that he had seen or sensed them. I could not read his face but when he said 'Okay' I believed he gave it the benefit of the doubt. All I knew was I wanted to honor God and honor leadership and give the Lord every opportunity to minister to people. I could feel the needs of the people pulling on my heart, so I did not care if the pastor thought I was crazy.

What happened next marked and changed my life. I felt a rushing wind come up behind my right shoulder. I knew it was not the Holy Spirit because I was already sensitive to what he was like (we will talk about this in a later chapter). I knew this wind was one of the angels that had been flying back and forth during the service. This angel tapped me on the shoulder and said, *'I am here for your breakthrough.'* The weight of those words was powerful and unforgettable. I did not know the name of that angel, and I knew nothing about DOS, but I knew a major shift in my life had begun. From the time that angel turned up I began going through inner healing and deliverance and supernatural things started happening to me. My prophetic gift increased, my faith increased, discerning increased, along with other spiritual gifts. I was so thankful for the words it spoke to me. After that encounter I regularly discerned the angels and much fruit came as a result.

There was a further increase in my DOS gift as a result of a dream where I saw rows of angels lined up. There seemed to be at least fifty of them of different sizes, shapes, and nationalities. I was amazed to see so many different types. In the dream I asked the question, 'Who in the world works with all these angels?' and I looked up to see the prophet Bob Jones standing in front of me. At that moment I woke up and felt God's presence. An impartation had taken place in the spirit realm. After that encounter I would feel the angels touching my right arm. That is how I discerned their presence with me. You may discern them in a whole different way. As I keep saying, every DOS gift is unique and every individual has their own language for it.

As I grew in discernment in this area I learned that angels have individual names, but that is a discussion for another time. At the moment I just want to chronicle the ways I learned to navigate this gift.

One day, I was sitting in Starbucks sipping on my coffee and writing, when I discerned an angel with me. This angel had to be at least 12 to 14 feet tall. I was astounded! I felt it standing there reading a scroll for about five minutes. I knew, even without him speaking, that he was there because of the call of God on my life. I knew it had to do with God setting me apart. I know now the angel was reading my destiny scroll. I was still new to this gift, but from that day there was an increase in deliverance anointing on my life.

Another time, my husband and I were grocery shopping and I felt the wind on my right shoulder. I asked the Holy Spirit, the teacher of all things, which angel was here. I was not asking its name but its function. And He said, "Healing". I do sometimes see angels via the SEER gift (1 Chronicles 29:29) but most times the way I function is to feel them on my arm. Holy Spirit switches it as He chooses. On this occasion, Holy Spirit having told me what angel was there, I turned around to the lady next to me in the grocery aisle and asked if she needed healing. I explained that I sometimes pray for people. She happened to be a Christian who had hurt her leg and hip in a fall the day before. We prayed for her and she was healed. Glory to Jesus! DOS is not so you can get puffed up in pride and say, "Oooh, look at me! I have this gift!" DOS is to be used to profit the Kingdom and bring God's agenda to this earth. When God's angels show up there is a divine purpose either to minister to you something to do with your calling, or to bring heaven to the people around you.

Quite often when I go out to eat, I will feel a particular angel. Its function is to bring revelation. As soon as I feel this angel the prophetic anointing opens up and I know that if I sit and listen I will get a prophetic word for the waiter. The first time this happened, discernment flowed easily, so that on subsequent occasions when I felt the same angel, it was easy for me to recognize that God wanted to speak to someone in the restaurant. I was not always excited about this. I am human. Sometimes I was tired from a busy day, or intent on enjoying family time, and when this angel would show up I would feel its weight and I really did not want to minister right then. But on these occasions, I remind myself that it's not about me and God's agenda is more important than my agenda. His heart is for the lost, the hurting, and the broken. So, I have to die to self and let Him release words into people's lives. He loves people and I shouldn't get in the way of that. Be assured there were also plenty of times when I was excited and happy to discern that angel! I am just telling you that the gift can manifest when you least expect it and that's when you have to prefer heaven's agenda over your own.

There is one specific restaurant encounter that made me appreciate how important it is to be obedient. On this occasion, I was already eating when I discerned the angel. God gave me a very long, detailed word. I went to the waitress to describe what was going on in her life as the Lord had showed me. I gave some very specific words about her son and what God was going to do in his life. She was almost in tears because she had been very concerned about him. A few months later, I was back in the same restaurant and that waitress came up and hugged me. She told me her life changed that day and she was so thankful for what had been spoken to her. I just smiled and told her God loves her, and then God gave her some more words!

People who work in restaurants are often in transition between jobs, going to college, or trying to work out what they want to do in life. It seems God sends me to those who are in transition, so that they will receive a directional word from Him at a time when they feel lost or confused. God shows me what they were born to do, and what their God-given talents and abilities equip them to do. I ask them if they have thought about that as a possibility and if I might pray with them. If they are not yet followers of Christ, I lead them to the Lord. If they are already in the Lord, I decree a shift in their careers and for a willingness to allow God to do that.

Even as I write this, I feel some people are afraid to discern angels for fear of being deceived. Let's break that off right now. Discerning angels is not about worshipping them.

Discerning angels is God's gift to facilitate what He wants to do on the earth. Angels are servants sent to help us do what He wants. (Hebrews 1:14)

Just say this aloud: *"Papa, I repent of any religious teaching that I have agreed with that has hindered any of my discerning of angels and may have prevented me from moving in my gift. I repent of fear and of agreeing with it. I come out of agreement with fear and religion and in Jesus name I command any demon of religion or fear to come out. I ask you, Holy Spirit, to fill my heart and mind with Yourself and Your thoughts. I declare that God's love is made perfect in my heart and that I am bold and fearless in those things He has called me to. Amen."*

Of course, we are meant to move in wisdom. Wisdom comes from the Lord and is to be found in His written Word. If an angel appears to you and asks you to do or say something that does not line up with the Word of God, then you will know that angel is a counterfeit. It is true that such counterfeits have brought widespread deception and given rise to whole religions. God has given us the wisdom of His Word to know when an angelic encounter is not from Him. When an encounter does not line up with His Word, then you know to command it to leave in Jesus name.

Now that we have addressed the specific things Holy Spirit put on my heart, here are a few more examples from my own experience of the operation of DOS and the angelic realm.

When I was working in the hospital I would pray as the Holy Spirit led. Normally, He would show me who I could pray for and who would be open to it. Over time, I discerned the angels with me only in respect to particular people. I knew by the Spirit when the angels' function was for healing. There were times I would pray the prayer of faith for people without feeling this healing angel, but I knew the anointing wasn't as strong.

This knowledge caused me to pay more attention to when that angel was there and when it wasn't. When it was, I could acknowledge it and thank God for sending it, and look to see what the Lord wanted me to do at that given moment. One day I was under the doctor's instruction to give a breathing treatment to a man who was having major heart issues. As I stepped out of the room to chart on the patient, I felt a very strong wind and felt the angel say, *"If you go and pray for him I will heal him."* Boy, was my faith increased as I prayed for that guy! I felt the power of God fill that room. That man was healed, praise God! God loves to do the impossible.

I discovered that I feel an increase in angelic activity in certain localities. For example, every time I go to California I seem to encounter a strong Angel of Revelation. My friend, who meets me at the airport and travels with me, will witness to this. During our time together I am able to tell her exactly when the angel turns up. When I know I have a prophetic word for a person, I don't have to press in for it. The words just came on the people with a weightiness that makes it so easy. Prophetic words would just roll out of me for passengers beside me on the plane, in the airport, at every restaurant, and in every store we entered.

Sometimes, at home, when my husband and I are worshipping together, I will start discerning this big angel of Glory that I see in the Seer realm. I know when that angel is present, because Glory increases in our house and we feel tangible glory in our bodies. When my husband and I were commissioned for service, I discerned a tall angel standing behind me. The person commissioning also discerned it. The angel was there in confirmation of the commissioning. It was a Grace Awakening angel assigned to our ministry so we could help people awake to that grace in their own lives.

When the Lord led me to record webinars we would feel particular angels during the teaching and impartations. There were even people watching later who saw and sensed them. I hope my experiences help you understand how this works, and that you keep a journal, as I did, so that you can note the different trends and patterns of angelic function. Remember, learning these things take time, but I declare acceleration over you as you read this, because God wants, and needs, you to function in the gift of DOS.

Even as I close out this chapter, the Holy Spirit is

reminding me that I have angels helping me to write it. Information regarding angels who help me when I write, was given to my husband in a Word of Knowledge, which is a different gift, and function, from DOS. The Lord told him I have three angels that work with me when I write. I am so thankful God sends his helpers to help me accomplish what Father wants done on the earth. Right now, you too could take time to thank the Lord. *"Lord, I thank you for your angels that you have assigned to me to help me walk in the call of God on my life. In Jesus' mighty name. Amen."*

Discerning the Holy Spirit

It's my delight and honor to write about discerning the Holy Spirit. I so enjoy Him. Let me share a few scriptures that speak of the amazing third person of the Godhead. He is a person, just like the Father and Jesus are persons. Unfortunately, He has not been talked, or taught, about enough, for people to have an effective grid for discerning Him. I realize certain streams of the Church do have, but for the sake of any new believer reading this, I want to cover some basics.

The Word says in John 14:26, *"The Holy Spirit who my Father will send in my name (in My place to represent Me and act on My behalf), He will teach you all things. And He will help you remember everything that I have told you."* WOW. He is all encompassing in so many ways. You could look up scripture after scripture on who He is, but I want to focus on discerning Him and how I learned to do that. Making and keeping a relationship with the Holy Spirit is no different to how you forge a relationship with any person; you spend time with Him in intimacy, acknowledging that He is both present and real.

Before we begin sharing some stories about the Holy Spirit, let's start with a simple prayer: "Holy Spirit, *I invite you to make yourself real to me. Please help me to know you, and be discerning of you and what you are doing around me."*

I like to refer to Holy Spirit as a gentleman. He likes to be invited and honored. Yes, there are times He comes in as a Lion, but most times I have chosen to invite Him. My relationship with Him was cultivated over time. I want to emphasize that, because as you grow with Him, He will cultivate so many things in your life. He is just as alive and active as the other two Persons of the Godhead, which is a truth of the Word that must not be denied. You will start discerning Him as you recognize and honor who He is. Discerning will flow from having spent time with Him. Because we all are unique in our design, it follows that your journey with Holy Spirit may differ from mine; the signal language between you may differ from mine. My own journey with Him began when I was baptized in the Holy Spirit, as clearly explained in the Bible: *"As they were filled with the Holy Spirit they began speaking in new tongues."* (Acts 2:3 NKJV)

I love how God knows exactly what we need. One day, knowing I needed to get my information from God, not man, I just prayed, *"Okay Lord, I have heard man's opinion on speaking in tongues. Now I want you to show me the truth. Is this from you? If so, I need you to show me in the Scriptures."* I was studying the Word and He highlighted Acts 19:2 to me. This is where Paul came to Ephesus and asked some believers if they received the Holy Spirit when they believed. They replied that they had been baptized into John's baptism of repentance, but they had not known that there was a Holy Spirit. Under Paul's ministry they went on to believe in Christ Jesus and were baptized in His name. When Paul laid hands on them, the Holy Spirit came on them and they began to speak with new tongues and to prophesy.

As I read this, a powerful revelation hit me. It was like a mighty river and God's lightning rod all at the same time! From that moment, speaking in tongues flowed from me. I found myself singing and praying in tongues all the time, even when I was driving my car. It became my passion to cultivate the Holy Spirit. I wish I could say this process was fast, but for me it wasn't. I needed much more impartation and revelation of who He was. I was still growing in character at that time, and I went through many trials. [1] I was faithful, though. Even as I write this, the Holy Spirit is showing me there is always a new measure of Him to experience - forever increasing, if we allow it.

In becoming more aware of Holy Spirit, we will learn what grieves Him, the Bible says that the Holy Spirit is grieved by sin and disobedience.

The Holy Spirit knows we can only go so far with Him if we only obey half of what He says. As my journey progressed, repenting of sins and receiving deliverance and inner healing, my relationship with Holy Spirit went deeper. I read books about Holy Spirit, and also invested time and money to receive impartation from leaders. I was faithful to spend time talking with Holy Spirit even if I did not get answers right away. Over the years I cultivated the different ways I could discern Him. I would feel Him all kinds of ways, but especially in my spiritual senses.

I will attempt to explain how I learned to discern His presence. I kept seeking to understand Him, and Holy Spirit would talk to me in various ways. As I prayed in the Spirit I would hear in my mind a strong voice. It would give me answers that I knew did not come from my natural intellect. It was different from Father God talking to me. It was louder, especially in the beginning when I was still unsure who was who. Then, as I began understanding and discerning him, I began to have open visions. Holy Spirit spoke to me through these visions, just as it was promised in Acts 2:17: "*I will pour forth of My Spirit...and your young men (or women) shall see visions."*

I highly recommend you take Patricia King's Class, *Knowing the Holy Spirit,*[2] in which she expounds the New Testament scriptures which outline the seventy functions of the Holy Spirit. She teaches that visions are the most common way of learning to discern Holy Spirit. The first vision I had was an open eyes vision of me as a strong warrior, in a white gown with a sword in my hand. In the vision I started speaking in tongues and my voice got louder and louder. Every time I spoke in tongues the devil was defeated. It was powerful to see the image of who I was in the Spirit and to have it line up with Ephesians 6:18, *"With all prayer and petition pray at all times in the Spirit, and with this in view, be on alert with all perseverance and petition for all the saints."* This is a way we can invite Holy Spirit and honor Him. You will discern Him more readily when you invite Him because by that very action you shift your focus onto Him.

Remember, the Holy Spirit is a spirit, so He isn't confined to time or space. At times, I would feel a tangible presence of God and discern it was Holy Spirit in the room with me. It would be so powerful and I was so thankful. He often wakes me up early in the morning to write or spend time in the Word before the house gets busy. He knows that is the time when He will have my full attention without the things of the world pulling on me. Sometimes, when I am preaching or teaching, I feel a mighty rushing wind show up in the room, heavy like it was at Pentecost. When I know I am discerning

Him, I always want to know *why* He is there. I ask the question: "What are You doing in this present setting and situation?"

Sometimes He shows up just to teach and guide me, other times He shows up to touch the people around me. Remember, we are to honor His ways. We may be used to discerning Him in a particular way, but then He switches it on us because He wants to reveal Himself in a way we have not explored. Learn your language in this process. Keep a journal, talk to Holy Spirit, and ask Him to help you to be discerning of Him continually. Love what He loves, hate what He hates. Enjoy the journey of discerning. Yes, I know it can be frustrating when you discern something but you're not sure what it is. I have been there many times, and the key to understanding is always to ask the Holy Spirit: what am I discerning about right now? What does He want to show me? He truly does teach us all things.

Another way discerning takes place for me is through fire. Luke 3:16 talks about the baptism of Holy Spirit and fire. I will be lying in bed and my body becomes so hot as the fire of God fills me over and over. This may be happening for several reasons. The Spirit of Holiness is a fire that burns out anything the Lord does not want in me. Sometimes it is a healing anointing going through me like a hot flame.

During deliverance sessions I rely heavily on the Holy Spirit and it's very easy to discern Him because He is quite blunt about naming what the person needs to be delivered from. At such times it's as though the power of God shoots out of me as described in Luke 4:18, *"The Spirit of the Lord is upon me to set at liberty those who are oppressed."* Also, Micah 2:13 KJV *"The breaker goes up before them; they break out, pass through the gate and go out by it. So their king goes on before them, and the Lord at their head."* These are the times I shake with the raw power of the Holy Spirit. It hits like a lightning rod. I know some people are very critical about shaking, but I say, judge by the fruit that results. I leave it up to Holy Spirit how He shows up; I just want Him to know He is invited. When Holy Spirit shows me a hidden matter of the enemy's sneak attack in someone's life, I know He will show up to break it. As I shake and command with words, Holy Spirit tears down the assignment and there is evidence the attack is broken. It's the way the breaker comes out of me. Don't dismiss a manifestation at any meeting you go to, but trust God to show you if there is any counterfeit in it.

Sometimes I discern Holy Spirit's presence by the ecstatic prophecy falling on me. At such times I realize the words coming out of my mouth are Heaven's words and they carry a different weight in the Spirit realm. If you are not sure what ecstatic prophecy is, I recommend Stacey Campbell's book about it.[3] Remember, this is a journey. I will say this multiple times through the book so that you don't fixate on how you were discerning Holy Spirit at first. Always let him do a new thing in you.

Right now, I feel the Holy Spirit is leading me to pray for you. *"I declare and decree that you will come to know Holy Spirit well, and you will be discerning of Him with a high sensitivity."*

There are times when discerning Him happens because I become fully immersed in Holy Spirit's emotions for the person I am ministering to. I start crying because I feel and sense the Holy Spirit's heart for that person's pain or sickness. I know these emotions are His because in the natural I wouldn't love a stranger that deeply or that quickly. I need to have Holy Spirit's heart to enable me to pray what He shows me at that moment.

I have come to enjoy discerning Him as He speaks in that still small voice that counsels me. It could be that He is calling me out on a heart attitude, or that He is affirming me in my identity. Sometimes, it is to show me how to partner with Him in order to fulfill a particular assignment here on earth. For example, this book was His idea and not mine. If I had not discerned that He was speaking to me, I would have missed it.

As you are reading this, Holy Spirit may be reminding you of some of the ways you discerned Him throughout your life, without you realizing it. Write them down now, and as you do, the Holy Spirit will begin to show you more, and new, ways of discerning Him.

As you partner with Him, you will find Him faithful.

How many of you have been in church services where the atmosphere felt dry and hard? Then you went to a church service somewhere else and you felt a whole different atmosphere of life and glory. Guess what? You were discerning the Holy Spirit! Understand, too, that if you suddenly smelled a sweet aroma that had no natural explanation, you could have been discerning by smell what Holy Spirit was doing at that moment in the room. An example might be when you smelt honey and it was at a time when you were receiving revelation on some aspect of the Word. That's discerning the Holy Spirit. I cannot tell you all the ways Holy Spirit may be discerned, nor do I want to. You are unique to Him and so is the relationship and language that you are developing with Him.

An easier way for you to discern the presence of Holy Spirit is when one of the nine gifts of the Spirit starts operating through you. Here's an example: I am preaching, and suddenly, out of nowhere, I feel a huge headache I didn't have before. I realize Holy Spirit is giving me a word of knowledge concerning someone's need for healing. At work one day I was taking a break with a co-worker. Suddenly, I felt a strong back pain and sensed Holy Spirit was revealing a word of knowledge to me so that He could touch my co-worker. I asked if she had back pain and she described to me what had caused it. I prayed for her and she was healed. If I had not discerned Holy Spirit and what He wanted to do, she would not have been healed at that time. I have learned to enjoy partnering with this gift because it helps so many people.

Partnering with Him in this way may come through intercession or flowing in DOS, or through any of the other gifts.

Sometimes discerning Him is His 'set up' to get you flowing in the other gifts. When I started sensing what felt like a river coming out of my belly, I discerned Holy spirit wanted me to give a word of prophecy. Then He caused me to flow in a "nabiy" word. James Goll describes the nabiy' as the action of "flowing forth."[4]

What I am explaining here is how DOS and the other gifts all intertwine. If I hadn't learned to discern when it is Holy Spirit, I would have just obsessed about those strange sensations I felt and withheld words of knowledge that helped people.

Holy Spirit will sometimes give you instructions in a still small voice. One time He spoke to me and told me not to eat whipped cream any more. I had cultivated a relationship with him by this time and I knew it was His voice, so I did what He said. There are times when I may ask him to explain, but at other times I just trust that He knows what is best for me. If you will honor Him, He will come. When you begin discerning Him it's for a purpose. It may just be to encourage you to spend time with Him. It could be there is someone He wants to minister to through you. It could be to have you know His heart for a situation and you weep and feel Him heavy like a weight. You surrender, and a deep desire comes on you to move into intercession.

There are thousands of ways Holy Spirit can help you be discerning of Him. Sometimes you just know in your "knower". You don't have to think about it, you just know its Holy Spirit, you act on it and there is good fruit from it. Get to know him through discerning Him and then partner with Him in what He is doing.

Many people have missed Him not just by not discerning Him, but by being afraid of Him. I don't want that to be you. That's why this chapter is in this book. Holy Spirit is key to walking in your divine destiny, but even when you begin discerning Him, He will not force you to partner with Him. He is a gentleman and He will respect your choice to flow with Him or shut Him down. I have seen that happen many times and it stalls your destiny.

My prayer is that having read only this much on the topic and begun to receive impartation of DOS, He will reveal even more of Himself to you. God knew we needed this part of the Godhead and that's why He sent him at Pentecost.

In my walk with Holy Spirit over the years, I understand it takes time for us to enter into a deeper relationship with him, just as it does with human relationships: for example, a newlyweds' intimacy level versus twelve years into marriage. By nurturing intimacy you will begin to understand more of the Holy Spirit's heart. You will know what makes Him happy and what grieves Him. As you navigate those things your discerning will transition into a place where you are more sensitive to what He is showing and highlighting to you. It was entirely Holy Spirit's idea that I partner with Him to write this book, just as it was He who taught me to walk in the gift of DOS. Without the gifts of the Spirit I could not do what He has called me to do. His gifts help me carry out the call of God on my life. I am forever grateful to Him.

If you want more of Holy Spirit you must honor him. Right now, you could just simply pray, *"Holy Spirit I honor you. Teach me and help me to be more intimate and more discerning of you."*

Discerning Human Spirits / Motives

What does it mean to discern human spirits? Stories with examples are one of the best ways to explain things. Jesus frequently used stories in His ministry. Human beings are three-part beings. Like an egg – shell, white and yolk - we are body, soul and spirit, made in the image of God - Father, Son and Holy Spirit. Once we are born again our true self is our spirit-man. That part of us is righteous and pure, a new creation, thanks to what Jesus Christ did on the cross. But our bodies and souls are not like that unless they come into submission to the Spirit of God.

Jesus was discerning of the motives behind what

people said. He discerned what was really in the hearts of the Pharisees and the Sadducees when they criticized Him for casting out demons. He said, '*You brood of vipers, how can you being evil, speak what is good? For the mouth speaks out of that which fills the heart.*' (Matt. 12:34-36). Have you ever heard a prophetic word, knowing it was a little "off" and that it was motivated more by the soul of the person rather than God's Spirit? It's kind of like that. Yes, we are called to love everybody, but if you walk alongside individuals who choose not to deal with their character flaws you may find they can open doors that put you at risk spiritually.

Let me give you an example: Someone gives you some advice and you ask the Lord for His wisdom about it. It is revealed to you that the advice came from their soul. It was not from the Lord, not from the Holy Spirit, but from their soul-man – their natural mind. I believe the born-again spirit is perfect, but it can be influenced, or filtered, by the mind, will and emotions of the soul which have not undergone renewal by the spirit. Discerning of human spirits is not a negative thing, it is necessary and strategic for healthy relationships. In the example I just described, you could use DOS as a key to intercession for the person who gave you soulish advice.

Other examples: Someone walks into the room and you sense a presence around him/her. Maybe that person is a leader with a very high calling, but you sense a crooked heart. You have just discerned who they are in the spirit realm; You have only just been introduced to a person and suddenly you have a vision in your mind's eye. You see that person writing a book with a special pen in their hand. God may be showing you that person was designed by Him to write, having been created with a natural ability to do that; I walk into the staff room and suddenly I hear in my head, *"Wow, April is working today. That's great! I enjoy working with her."* You wonder why you are picking up your colleague's thoughts. It is not demonic talk, or a demon or an angel or the Holy Spirit or the Lord, but your colleague's spirit man that you are discerning.

This has happened to me so often. Sometimes it really confuses me because I feel their thoughts like they are my own. Here is a really confronting example of this. I am out in a crowd somewhere and I hear these thoughts, *"Man, that guy over there is hot. I really hope he asks me out. Maybe if I wait here he will come over."* Now, I personally am happily married and have no problem with lust. I know myself and I don't struggle with thoughts like that. So I look around me and beside me there is a beautiful woman who is staring at a man in the center of the room. Well, bingo! now I know I am discerning her spirit-man.

This area of gifting can get awkward sometimes because it feels like your own thoughts, and that can be heavy at times. You will need to know yourself very well. When you know it's not an area that you have issues with, then know that you are discerning someone else's issue. Some people have a way of successfully navigating this part of discerning, but

71

some may end up mentally distressed because they have not learned what gift they have, or how to steward it with Holy Spirit. With this gift, as with any other of the gifts, the Holy Spirit may bring an increase in it and there will be a learning curve at each new level. Be kind to yourself in this process. Ask the Lord to give you a friend who walks in this gift - one who is trustworthy and with good character. You guys can then run the race together and strengthen each other by swapping stories of the weird things that happened at the market today!

It's important, also, to ask the Lord for clean hands and pure heart in this area. You may be discerning people who want to use you, take advantage of you, betray you, think very negative things about you in their minds. What do you do with all that information? You talk to the Lord about it and you allow Him to show you how to use the information He gives you. Stay humble and let the love of God be shed abroad in your heart. God gifts you with the ability to discern human spirits for many different reasons and one of them is to teach you to love well, regardless of what you're discerning about them. No matter what God shows you, you must walk in the fear of the Lord. Always carry His heart for people, or you may become hardened and cold as you see evil intentions, negativity, or selfish motives.

When someone who has wrong motives wants to use you, remember Jesus went through the same thing. Jesus knew what was in the heart of the treasurer of His close group of twelve. He knew Judas was a self-seeking thief, and yet He still loved him. I have had people come up to me and say they want to be a part of my ministry. Unfortunately, they didn't come with a servant's heart to help me, but with a desire for self-promotion. It happens, folks! People are people and we're are all at different stages of growth and character refinement. The sad thing is such people are ultimately robbing themselves. If they would stop focusing on being promoted they would fulfil their assignments in God and be amazed at what God does through them. The truth is, promotion comes only from the Lord. God made each one of us to be history changers who will always take time to celebrate one another's successes on the journey.

You will sometimes sense things you wish you hadn't. Imagine this scenario: You are out to dinner with a good friend and her husband. You are pleased to meet her husband because she is always saying how amazing he is. But you are barely seated before you are discerning an adulterous affair. Her husband is intent on engaging your attention. You are overwhelmed by the emotions of the affair flashing off in your head. It's so loud it's hard to focus on the conversation around the dinner table. You try to act normally, but you are shocked this is happening to a friend you love so dearly. Her husband starts asking you questions about yourself, and all the while you realize you are discerning his character. You keep taking sips from your glass, trying to keep your composure, but finally, you excuse yourself and escape to the restroom. You take it to the Holy Spirit to ask how he wants you to handle what you have just seen. Does He want you to repent for this man and pray for a change of heart? Does He want you to tell your best friend? How will you handle your friendship if you are told to do nothing?

This is where you learn not to judge, but to cultivate, even more, your relationship with Holy Spirit. He will help you walk out your gifting through situations such as I described above. It may be uncomfortable knowing what's happening in that situation, but there is a reason He showed you and you must take that seriously. You can love and bless people at a distance, but you may not want to double date! The polar opposite to the above situation is when God shows you someone whose heart is so pure. From the moment you meet them, you just know they are clean before the Lord and you can trust them. It is so refreshing when God allows you to see that. It's a beautiful thing, too, to see when someone has been restored by the Lord. Celebrate those times.

"Lord, I ask that you give everyone reading this chapter clean hands, a pure heart, and a grace to love despite what they may discern. I decree they will not be judgmental or critical, but will live redemptively."

Discerning Demons

You may have picked up this book because you are already conscious of this gift, having already discerned demons from time to time. You may be ready to learn more, or you may be really concerned at what it means and where it will lead.

I have found some people give in to fear when it comes to this aspect of discerning. God has not given you a spirit of fear, but peace and a sound mind (2 Tim. 1:7) and so I pray you will read this chapter free of any torment. Please pray this prayer before you read on.

"Lord, I repent for having any fear of demons. I command any spirit of fear out of me even from my time in the womb. Holy Spirit come fill those places. Greater is He that is in me than He that is in the world. Amen, so be it!"

According to Luke 10:19 KJV, you have been given *"All authority to trample on snakes and scorpions and to overcome all the power of the enemy, and nothing will harm you."* Jesus Christ paid the price on the cross for you to be sons and daughters who move on earth in the authority that He has given you. If you see or discern a demon, ask the Holy Spirit how to deal with it. Do you cast it out of the person, command it out of a house you're visiting, or is it a ruling spirit in the region? Always dialogue with the Holy Spirit about what you are discerning.

This gift is so effective in deliverance ministry. You can discern what needs to be commanded off, or out of, a person in order for them to be set free. This is a very important ministry of the Holy Spirit. Because Jesus Christ came to set the captives free it is an essential part of doing Kingdom business. It was not until later in life that I experienced deliverance and I do not want the next generation to have to wait that long. Imagine if this generation could experience their inheritance of deliverance early in their Christian walk! How much more effective they will be for the advancement of the Kingdom! That's my prayer. This book is not about debating whether or not a Christian can have demons. If you want to explore that topic look up one of the many Derek

Prince videos on YouTube, which will give you sound Biblical evidence.

You can discern demons through any of your senses. You can taste, sense, smell, hear, or see them. Because of the environment I grew up in I was particularly sensitive to demonic activity and God had to grow me so that I became more balanced. I have found this to be the case with many people who are strong in this gift. Satan hates them and their gifting. He knows they will uncover the hidden things he doesn't want exposed, and for that reason he takes every opportunity to oppress them, even from childhood, or to lead them into some form of counterfeit spirituality.

In the early stages of developing this gift you may be discerning of a demon without immediately knowing its name or function. When I started moving in deliverance I would discern the presence of demons as I put my hands on someone. The person would often scream as the fire of God pushed the demons out. At that time, I did not know the names of the demons.

Another time, during deliverance ministry in my house, the fire of God pushed all the demons out, but one hid in my dog. Three days later it spoke to me from the dog, saying, "Who do you think you are, casting me out?" That so shocked me it took me a couple of days to remember the same thing happened when Jesus cast out the demons from the madman called Legion. The demons spoke, begging Jesus to allow them to inhabit the nearby herd of pigs (Mark 5:2-13 NASB). Now, I have more understanding and I know to spiritually "sweep my house" and not allow the demons to hide.

Allow for God's grace on yourself as you learn. You do not come out of the gate knowing everything there is to know about the ministry of discernment. Trust the Holy Spirit to train you. He will guide you and give you the revelation to bring His Kingdom on earth. As I grew in this gift, I would discern through Holy Spirit what demons to cast out. Holy Spirit would give me their names as I asked Him to help me discern the "strongman" that smaller demons attach themselves to. Let me give you an example. Fear is a strongman, a stronghold. But a bunch of other spirits will attach themselves to that: abandonment, abuse, rejection, the list can be long. With the gift of DOS in operation, the deliverance minister is enabled to identify and uproot the demonic strongholds in people's lives. If your desire is to be effective in God's army of deliverers, but you don't yet have the gift of DOS, now is the time to ask Him for it.

There are always opportunities to gain understanding. Let's say you move in the gift of healing. You start praying for someone concerning the constant pain in their right arm. Suddenly, you sense a spirit of affliction and infirmity. You tell that thing to get out in Jesus name, and before your eyes, that person is healed! Say one of your family members unexpectedly chews you out. Initially, you are stunned, but then you see a demon of hate and anger. Right then and there you know what is happening. The Holy Spirit may have you interceding for this person's freedom. Sometimes you see in order to shut it down and forbid it to operate around you. Other times you may see, hear, taste or feel it, and be of assistance to someone else to cast it out.

Another example: You could be driving across state borders and suddenly you see this 40-foot demon, and you see it exercises power over the whole state or region. It may not be your personal assignment to take that thing out, but you *can* forbid it to operate while you are there. No matter what you are discerning, greater is He that's in you than he that is in the world. You have all power to trample over demons. Do not allow them to scare you or intimidate you. They have to go in the name of Jesus Christ.

You will learn to trust the Holy Spirit to show you what you *need* to see. Ask the Holy Spirit for an increase of this gift, and that he would reveal any hidden thing in your own life or in the lives of people close to you, because this is a means of protection, particularly if you are in leadership. It may reveal witches who have infiltrated your circle of associates, or Jezebel attacks and assignments. People are reluctant to acknowledge and discuss this issue, but it's real. Much wisdom is needed to walk and flow in this gift.

More than in any other time in history, this is the time that the body of Christ needs to be discerning. We are at war whether you choose to participate or not. If you do not take a stand against the devil and his cohorts you will have made a choice by default. He roams the earth seeking whom he may devour, but it doesn't have to be you. DOS is to be used for the extension of God's Kingdom. If the Holy Spirit shows you someone who has a demon of rejection, abandonment, or abuse, then He wants you to pray for that person, or possibly cast it out.

Earlier, I mentioned that DOS can make you super sensitive to witchcraft and perversion. When those spirits are present all your senses come into play and your body may react very strongly. Some people feel a tightening in their stomach. Some get an intense headache. So intense is their resistance to that spirit they may feel anger to the point of wanting to fight. Learning to navigate this will involve patience, time, and help from your mentor. Many have experienced these extreme reactions in dealing with this sinister spirit. I think it's God's warning system to protect you. Remember, we do not war against flesh and blood, but against principalities. In Jesus we have all power over the devil.

A word of caution: you don't go looking for the spirit of witchcraft and accusing people of it. Don't fall into suspicion and false accusation. There are times you will know that you know, but it is imperative that you ask Holy Spirit what to do about it. Take authority in forbidding that spirit to operate around you until God shows you how to pray for that individual. Keep in mind that this spirit is often generational, having begun in the individual's family line, so do not judge. Only God knows the heart of the individuals who are willing to be set free. Nothing is too big, or longstanding, that He cannot deliver.

I had a dream one time about a person carrying a Jezebel, or witchcraft, spirit. In the dream God said to me, *"Do you think that's too difficult for Me?"* I knew the answer to *that* question! It is important that you are diligent to always carry this gift with clean hands and a pure heart, (Psalm 24:3-4) for God wants to use DOS to bring protection for the Body of Christ and redeem bloodlines. We'll talk more about that later, but right now I do want to talk about sensitivity to perversion, male or female. You will have to be aware of your own personal discerning language to know how you may feel this spirit. Put me in a roomful of people, and I can tell you who is carrying sexual demons. This is not so I can make judgements, but in order for me to be aware. I raise this topic because, if your DOS sensitivity to these things is high, there will be times when you don't know how to handle it. You will be susceptible to what I call, "DOS overload". You need trustworthy people to pray for you and your overloaded nervous system, even if they don't understand all of your gifting. I know people who have carried this gift for years and still need occasional help in this area.

Jennifer Eivaz says you gain muscle in this gift[1], given time. Gaining spiritual muscle is an excellent way to think of it. The wonderful thing about this area of ministry is that you bring about great breakthrough in people's lives. Even for members of your own family you can pray for hidden things to be revealed so they can be set free. This gift is powerful in discerning generational curses that were hatched in the demonic realm and attached to bloodlines. With DOS you may very quickly discern any number of root causes of curses, such as murder, abuse, or abandonment. Many people go through a life of hell brought on by generational curses. There is a long list of generational curses that are in bloodlines…but GOD! Curses are broken and overcome by the blood of Jesus Christ. Sometimes it is useful to break the curses tied, or connected, to people's surnames.

More often than not the gift of DOS is not celebrated because it is the least understood. DOS is a sword to set captives free, break off every generational curse and uproot every demon. You are needed for the task, so take courage, particularly when this gift is hard for you to navigate. I declare a new grace over you for DOS right now. Holy Spirit wants to affirm you and encourage you to keep on pursuing and stirring up this gift. It's no different than stirring up the gift of prophecy or the gift of healing. Pray in the Spirit for the Holy Spirit to make it razor sharp in you. As you are faithful and remain pure, you will see great increase of clarity in the gift.

I celebrate you in your gift of DOS. I bless you as a co-laborer and declare you will be effective and sharp in it. May God help you to plunder the gates of hell for God's Kingdom.

Discerning the Glory

Those who walk strongly in DOS are usually very sensitive to atmospheres and are quick to discern the heavyweight of God's presence. It is possible to recognize the glory even if you do not have the gift of DOS, but people gifted in DOS are likely to be extra sensitive to the glory realm. I am very conscious that Holy Spirit wants me to write that.

So what does one feel in the Glory? I have heard it described in many ways. Some say it feels like rain coming into a room, like a light mist. Others describe it as a thick, warm cloud because it feels like the love of God is in their very being. Others have described it as a burning fire, or a vibration of His glory. Some people describe it as a deep, revelatory realm, when the atmosphere seems so thick and tastes of honey. Sometimes I just wake up feeling warmth, like a bubble, around me. That's the best way I can describe the glory of His presence. When it happens I know He is romancing me to spend time getting to know Him and ministering to Him.

It's not our job to judge these experiences, or esteem one more than another; instead, look at the fruit in the lives of people who have the glory manifest around them.

In reality, we were all made to experience His glory and Christ is the access point to enter into this realm, but *DOS allows you to discern when glory is on someone else.* If you desire to know more about the glory realm there are many books which teach on the subject, but this chapter is simply to acknowledge and illustrate how DOS enables you to *discern* the glory of God's presence. There are people I meet and right away I can see a thick haze around them and I immediately know they are people of His presence. I know they take time to soak in the presence of God and carry his glory. It is so refreshing to be discerning of this.

Sometimes when you are discerning His glory it's an invitation to go dine with Him, like the scripture says: "Behold, I stand at the door and knock; if anyone hears my voice and opens the door, I will come in to him and will dine with him and he with me." (Rev. 3:20) NKJV. If you are already walking in this gift of DOS, I declare a new sensitivity in you to be discerning of His glory. God wants you to experience and enjoy it. My next book will be all about His glory, but it is no accident that you are reading this one. I pray it makes you hungry for even more of God and His glory realm. Be like Moses and ask the Lord to show you His glory (Exodus 33:18). It is a request He loves to answer.

Lord, may everyone who is reading this right now experience your presence, especially if it's for the first time. "According to their heart desire, Lord, show them Your glory".

Closing Thoughts

I have included discussion questions in this chapter.

CHAPTER ONE DISCUSSION

What Is Discerning of Spirits?

1. Define what this gift is and write it down in order to keep it in the forefront of your mind. Ask the Holy Spirit to increase your sensitivity in discerning.

   _____

   _____

   _____

   _____

2. Take the time to ask the Holy Spirit where this gift has already been active in your own life, and write down anywhere where it has gone unnoticed.

   _____

   _____

   _____

   _____

CHAPTER TWO DISCUSSION

Help, What Do I Feel?

1. What will your first response be when you discern something, and you're not sure how to handle it? Write it down.

    _____

    _____

    _____

    _____

2. What support systems do you have in place to help you when you have an over a discerning day? List a few responses below.

    _____

    _____

    _____

    _____

CHAPTER THREE DISCUSSION

Discerning the Angels

1. How has the Holy Spirit activated you to discern angels? Remember, we are all unique individuals, and you may discern them differently than other people discern them.

   _____

   _____

   _____

   _____

2. Track the purposes of the angels you begin discerning, then ask the Holy Spirit to reveal something new to you about that angel.

   _____

   _____

   _____

   _____

CHAPTER FOUR DISCUSSION

Discerning the Holy Spirit

1. Pray and ask the Holy Spirit to help you be more sensitive to Him. List the ways you were more sensitive to Him this week.

   _____

   _____

   _____

   _____

2. Begin to cultivate conversations with the Holy Spirit and record a few responses here.

   _____

   _____

   _____

   _____

CHAPTER FIVE DISCUSSION

Discerning Human Spirits/Motives

1. Have a predetermined way you will respond when you discern bad motives that will keep your heart pure.

   _____

   _____

   _____

   _____

   Write a commitment to yourself below.

   _____

   _____

   _____

   _____

2. Pray prayers of love and selflessness over other

people's human motives you discerned this week, to bless them. Record them below.

_____

_____

_____

_____

CHAPTER SIX DISCUSSION

Discerning Demons

1. Write down three demons you discerned this week, and how you discerned them.

   _____

   _____

   _____

   _____

2. As Holy Spirit is training you, remember that not everything you see is your assignment to do something about. Ask Holy Spirit why you saw this particular demon and record the answers below.

CHAPTER SEVEN DISCUSSION

Discerning the Glory

1. Commit to several times this week that you will be intentional to get in the Lord's presence and praise Him. Write them below.

   _____

   _____

   _____

   _____

2. How did you most commonly feel or experience His awesome presence?

   _____

   _____

   _____

   _____

Notes

Chapter 1: What Is Discerning of Spirits?

1. https://en.wikipedia.org/wiki/Discernment
2. Jennifer Eivaz, Seeing The Supernatural, chapter. 2 (Grand Rapids, Michigan: *Chosen Books*, 2017]

Chapter 2: Help, What Do I Feel?

1. Gateway to my Miracle by April Stutzman [Self Published.: April Stutzman, 2018]

   Amazon: https://amzn.to/3mhHSjz
2. Jennifer Eivaz, Seer & Prophet Institute in person, 2018 10/25/2018

Chapter 4: Discerning the Holy Spirit

1. Patricia King, Glory School, https://pki.xpmedia.com/p/updated-glory-school
2. Stacy Campbell, Ecstatic Prophecy, (Grand Rapids, MI: Chosen Books, 2008)
3. Nabiy' according to James Goll, Discovering The Seer In You, (Shippensburg, Pen.: Destiny Image, 2007)

Chapter 6: Discerning Demons

1. Jennifer Eivaz, Seer & Prophet Institute in person, 2018 10/25/2018

About the Author

April Stutzman is co-founder with her husband Richard Stutzman of Kingdom Flame Ministries. She is a powerful deliverance minister and prophetic voice. April shares the heart of the Father to see people walk into wholeness and activated in their destiny. Currently, April and Richard are equipping the body of Christ through webinars and meetings. They love to activate people in healing, prophetic, and deliverance ministry.

To find out more about April and her ministry, you can visit her online:
Website: https://www.kingdomflameministries.com/

Youtube: April Stutzman Glory Stories

https://www.youtube.com/channel/UCXoI2CxV0L8VzXsQe PiGq4Q

Youtube: April Stutzman – Kingdom Decree's

https://www.youtube.com/channel/UCDLLFs3ATuzsMt-4UG2At7Q

Facebook: https://www.facebook.com/aprilrstutzman

Blog: https://www.kingdomflameministries.com/blog

Here are other podcast Feeds to Glory Stories.

Apple Podcast:

https://podcasts.apple.com/us/podcast/glory-stories-by-april-stutzman/id1478437594

Google Podcast:

https://www.google.com/podcasts?feed=aHR0cHM6Ly9hbm
Nob3IuZm0vcy9kNjhkZTc0L3BvZGNhc3QvcnNz

Spotify:

https://open.spotify.com/show/1V0QfXSSTJP8Xn1miwr9Yl

Stitcher:

https://www.stitcher.com/podcast/anchor-podcasts/glory-stories-by-april-stutzman

Breaker:

https://www.breaker.audio/glory-stories-by-april-stutzman-1

Pocket Cast:

https://pca.st/x6tDqK

Other Accounts:

Twitter: @bluizzforchrist
Periscope: @bluizzforchrist
Instagram: iamaprilstutzman

Address: Kingdom Flame Ministries
PO Box 7
Hendersonville, NC 28792

More Powerful Resources from April Stutzman

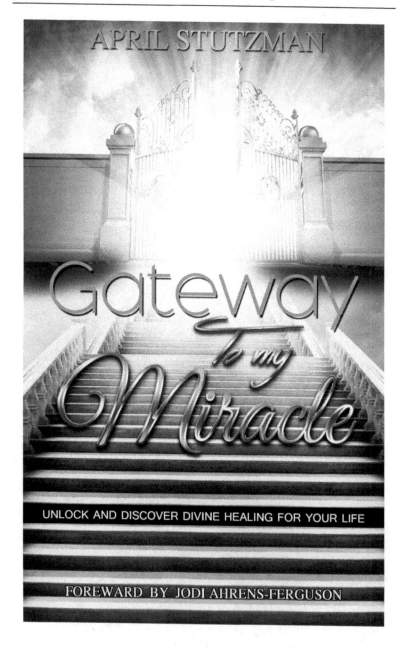

In **Gateway To My Miracle**, April details the process that Holy Spirit walked her through in receiving a miracle breakthrough. From personal experiences to debilitating fibromyalgia, she shares the revelation process of discovering and encountering a good God. This is the story of how God changed one woman from the inside out and transformed her life physically and emotionally. This book is a testimony of Jesus Christ, the healer. Her story will give you the keys to unlock the gateway to your miracle.

Here is the link or URL to this book.

https://amzn.to/3mhHSjz

We have a large print for you all!

https://amzn.to/2TkJ21g

April's book, **Gateway To My Miracle**, is a very transparent testimony of her upbringing. She shares how the Lord brought her through, even though she had no idea it was Him at that time. This story will inspire others to "not give up" but to believe God's Word that we can look to Him to use our past to shape us & prepare us for His Call & Destiny on our lives. You will gain helpful "tools for life" as you read April's story. Be Blessed & empowered.

Constance J. Bounds - God's Eagles Ministry

Gateway To My Miracle is the powerful testimony of April Stutzman's personal journey to healing. Far more than just the transparent sharing of a life-changing testimony, **Gateway To My Miracle** boldly addresses questions and misconceptions that surface in the body of Christ as well as outside of the church. Whether you are experiencing the need for physical or emotional healing yourself or are taking up the mantle to battle for others, you will find that this book is a faith builder and a powerful resource. This book will greatly benefit both you and those you care about. May God increase your faith and give you victory!

Jodi Ferguson - Co-Founder

Co-Director Warriors Heart Ministry, Women's Equipping Network, Producer of TV Show "Signs Following with JC"

I loved this book. Her testimony is amazing. Her healing and journey with God are exciting to read about. I have already read it twice. Easy to understand and receive your own miracles.

Sherry Boyd

In this book, April talks about her journey of healing, both inner healing and miraculous healing from fibromyalgia. I had heard a podcast interview with April, and from her brief testimony I heard, I knew I had to read this book. The book did not disappoint. A few quotes from the book that resonated with me. "I needed inner healing and deliverance. Why was this not being talked about and taught? "There was a wound in my soul, and deliverance was needed. Oh, how I wish the church would talk about this stuff and allow the Holy Spirit to make people whole. "A person can only love at the level their heart has received healing and love from God."

And then when God healed her from fibromyalgia, she heard God say: "If I can heal the nations, what kind of God would I be if I didn't heal you?" Wow! Just wow!

Joanna Russell

This book was so exciting to read because April told her life story of a lot of heartbreak and pain, realizing that God loves her so much and comes to her revealing His love through vision, healing her heart, healing her body, and she in faith goes forward and lets the Holy Spirit teach her as she reads the Word and receives more vision, and she now can teach and tell others of the Lord!

Pat Tranter

Gateway to My Miracle is April Stutzman's powerful testimony of Christ's redeeming love and miraculous power! As you read, April walks you through her own personal journey into healing and freedom. Her words ordained by Heaven and revelation from the Father will help set you free from the lies of the enemy, past trauma, and physical pain. If you are in need of keys for a breakthrough in your own life, then this is the book for you. As April shares her own emotional wounds of the past and infirmity, it will open your eyes and awaken your heart to the deep and hidden things in your own soul that Jesus wants to heal and deliver you from. This book had me searching my own heart as I read it. Get ready to unlock the gateway to the miracle you have been praying for!

Teryn Yancey
Co-founder of Glory Culture International

Freedom Sessions-Internal Healing

My husband and I enjoy ministering internal healing through Freedom Sessions online through Zoom or Google Meet Video. These sessions are generally two-hours long. Christ came to set the captives free, and we have received this mantle from the Lord. Our desire is to see each one walking in their God-given destiny. Over time wounds happen, cycles take place, and generational sin affects the bloodline. When we appropriate the power of the cross on the DNA, we bring victory to generational bloodlines for the purpose of carrying the glory. It is our most profound passion to see bloodlines restored to God's original intent. Following is a list of a few of the areas we have ministered to. There are many more.

Molestation	Rape
Trauma	Freemasonry
Abuse	History of cultism
Rejection	Orphan
Abandonment	Anger
Sexuality	Fear
Demons	Attack in Dreams

We have ministered to a lot of prophets and prophetic people by the mantle of the Lord. It is highly significant, as an Oracle of God, to deal with all issues of the heart so that they cannot contaminate your voice. The lens that we see and hear the Father through is related to our foundation. When we walk through the process of healing, we begin to make our foundation solid in Jesus Christ.

We celebrate Jesus Christ! Because of Him, we are able to set captives free and bind up the wounds.

If you have not accepted Jesus Christ as your personal Savior, please pray this prayer:

"Jesus, I believe you died on the cross for me and for my sin (areas that I have missed the mark). Forgive me of my sins, cleanse me, and wash me. I believe you died and were resurrected for me. Please make Yourself known to me. Amen."

Personal Testimonies

I would love to thank Richard and April for their love and care. When I met them and began a prayer, I felt like a family automatically. I've received so much breakthrough without even trying to do so. My family has also seen healing through my healing!

KB

Here is one of the testimonies of an SRA person that we have ministered too.

Some of us go through life with problems that we cannot seem to get over. We know somehow that there are issues that need to be resolved but have no idea where to start. I am so thankful for April and Richard for their diligence in studying and becoming knowledgeable in areas that are so horrible that most people do not want to deal with them. Because of their Freedom Sessions, I am experiencing freedom in areas that I thought I would never be free in. I have hope, I have peace, and more and more, I am walking in my true identity. I am extremely thankful to my Savior and Deliverer and for His servants, April, and Richard, for ministering freedom to the captives. There is hope!

Anonymous

My sessions with April and Richard have been transformative on many levels, some of which I am certain I haven't even seen the fullness of yet. They do incredible work in the spirit realm! I've been able to both learn from their methods as well as simply receive healing and deliverance through their prayers. Most importantly, my sessions with them have increased my awareness of my authority and have grown me in the confidence of who the Lord has created me to be. Their prophetic discernment has offered a lot of confirmation and encouragement to me. I've felt fear being dismantled, generational strongholds being shaken, and self-doubt and self-condemnation dissolve. Thank you, Jesus!

Love you guys, Allie

April's freedom sessions have been incredible!! I've had generational curses broken off. I feel more sensitive to the leading of the Holy Spirit and increase in the presence of the Lord!! Also, my Christian mother was tormented by demons for years!! This torment was removed through April being a seer by the power of the Holy Spirit!! She has been set free from years of what I thought were mental problems, but she saw it in the spirit! Wow, these were real demonic activities operating in my mother's life so thankful for April and her husband, Richard!!!

Hal

The most freeing thing I have experienced through the freedom sessions is the space to be open and discuss my "issues" and not feel judged. To understand, I am not crazy, and there is a solution. Jesus cares about every single little detail of my life (thoughts, emotions, and experiences), and I can fully trust and believe in Him to set me free from anything that hinders me from moving forward into my destiny!

Christy

Contact Information for Freedom Session-Internal Healing. Email: info@kingdomflameministries.com

Website:
https://www.kingdomflameministries.com/deliverance

We have 2-hour session rates.

We wanted you to know that my ebook is available on many platforms including these.

Apple, Amazon, Kindle, Google Play, Kobo,
Walmart Ebook, Nook, Itunes, and more!

Kingdom Flame T-Shirts Website
Design and other items for sale!

https://kingdomflame.threadless.com/

Kingdom Flame Ministries Resource Center!

https://www.kingdomflameministries.com/resources

Introduction to Deliverance

- Topics Discussed:
- What is deliverance
- Who needs deliverance?
- Reasons why deliverance is needed
- How do I start the process of deliverance?
- Basics of beginner's deliverance ministry
- Impartation & Activation

6 Things that Hinder's your Prophetic Flow

- Topics Discussed:
- Discussion on what the bible says about prophecy
- Activations
- What are prophetic acts
- What are 6 things that can hinder your prophetic voice
- Prayer and impartation

Carving a realm In Joy by April Stutzman

- Topics include:
- What is true, Joy?
- How do we walk in joy during the midst of hard places?
- Why is Joy a weapon?
- How to allow Joy to impact those around us?
- Is Joy a weapon?
- How did David express Joy?
- What are some of the Invaluable lessons of joy?

Prophetic Equipping by April Stutzman

- Topic includes:
- Prophetic ministry verses the office of a prophet
- Common attacks that try to hinder the prophetic flow in your life
- Overcoming hindrances in the prophetic
- Prophetic ministry times with Q and A
- Prophetic activation
- What is a seer prophet?

April Stutzman and Jodi -Dream Interpretation

- Topics include:

- The Basics – what does the bible say about dreams?

- Type of Dreams (warning, revelation, etc.) & Source of Dreams (God / not God)

- Dream Symbols & Tools & Interpretative Strategies

- Interpreting Other People's Dreams

Internal Healing of the Soul by April Stutzman and Patricia Doty

- Topic Covered:
- Abandonment - Abuse
- Orphan Spirit
- Trauma - Fear - PTSD
- Betrayal - Offences
- Unforgiveness - Suicide
- Restfulness - Bitterness
- Impartation and ministry times

Gifts of Discerning of Spirits

- Topics include:

- What is discernment, and why do I need it?

- Discerning human spirit

- Discerning the Angels

- Discerning the fallen demonic Angles

- Pitfalls of discerning -

- Impartation and Q and A sessions

- What is discernment, and why do I need it?

- Discerning human spirit Discerning the Angel's Discerning the fallen demonic Angles

- Pitfalls of discerning -Impartation and Q and A sessions

When you have a second to leave a review on the Amazon website, we would appreciate it. It also helps the ranking for my book, so others would be encouraged to buy it.

Please click on the links below and leave one. Nallie, our youngest daughter, would appreciate it as well. Bow Wow!

Amazon.com/review/create-review?&asin=1735175188

Amazon.com/review/create-review?&asin=1735175161

Blessing, *April*

The best way to thank an author is to write a review.

Audio books are on Apple, Amazon, Audible, Kobo, Google Play, Nook and More! CD Available on our Website.

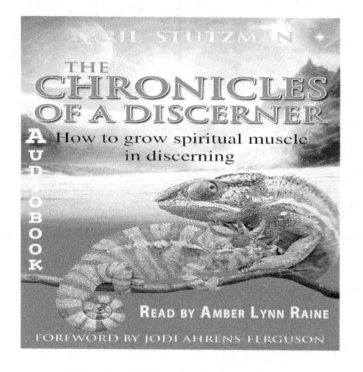

Free Audio Preview of Chapter 2

https://www.youtube.com/watch?v=NlNbKQIyUtg

Audio Music Endorsement Link Below:

https://youtu.be/ruWWY8VHVZ8

Audio books are on Apple, Amazon, Audible, Kobo, Google Play, Nook and More! CD Available on our Website.

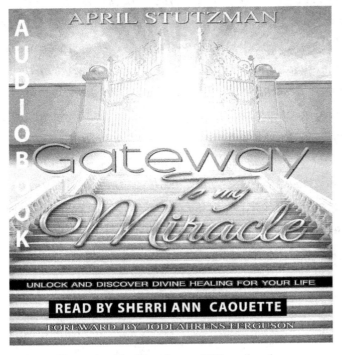

Free Audio Preview of Chapter 1:

https://youtu.be/GKoMvvmfl8Q

Audio Music Endorsement Link Below:

https://youtu.be/a6mwPGQc3bY

Prayer for Impartation

The Holy Spirit wants me to declare such precision to your Discerning of Spirits right now. *"Papa, in this season, I decree and declare to those reading this, that precision is happening in their gift. Their discernment will be razor-sharp! We cut off, right now, every assignment of error or mixture to contaminate the gift in Jesus' name. The wind of the Holy Spirit is present with you to move you into the new and help you let go of any staleness of the last season. I sense for some people that the disappointment that they have felt in the past has hindered their gift. I command all disappointment to go; all heaviness be gone now, in Jesus' name. All sorrow and grief go! I release the joy of the Lord and ask you, Papa God, to send the ministering angels to them."*

In Jesus Mighty name,

April.

Invite April to Speak at your next Event

April Stutzman is a powerful and anointed speaker and minister. She is an equipper, a prophetic trainer, and carries a strong inner-healing and deliverance mantle. If you would like to have April speak at your event, please send an email with requested dates and times to:

info@kingdomflameministries.com.

Topics Include:

Discerning of Spirits

Dream Interpretation

Prophetic Equipping

Carving a Realm of Joy

Introduction to Deliverance

Internal Healing of the Soul

6 things that will hinder your prophetic flow